W9-CAL-504

SUSTAINABLE WORLD

FOOD AND FARMING

Rob Bowden

**KIDHAVEN
PRESS**™

THOMSON
—✦—
GALE

OAK BROOK PUBLIC LIBRARY
600 OAK BROOK ROAD
OAK BROOK, IL 60523

San Diego • Detroit • New York • San Francisco • Cleveland
New Haven, Conn. • Waterville, Maine • London • Munich

© 2004 by KidHaven Press. KidHaven Press is an imprint of The Gale Group, Inc.,
a division of Thomson Learning, Inc.

KidHaven™ and Thomson Learning™ are trademarks used herein under license.

For more information, contact
KidHaven Press
27500 Drake Rd.
Farmington Hills, MI 48331-3535
Or you can visit our Internet site at http://www.gale.com

ALL RIGHTS RESERVED.
No part of this work covered by the copyright hereon may be reproduced or used in any form or by any means—graphic,
electronic, or mechanical, including photocopying, recording, taping, Web distribution or information storage retrieval
systems—without the written permission of the publisher.

Commissioning Editor: Victoria Brooker
Book Designer: Jane Hawkins
Consultant: Dr. Rodney Tolley
Hodder Children's Books
A division of Hodder Headline Limited
338 Euston Road, London NW1 3BH

Book Editor: Margot Richardson
Picture Research: Shelley Noronha, Glass Onion Pictures

Cover: A worker picking tea on a tea plantation in Java, Indonesia.

Picture credits: Cover: Denis Waugh/Getty Images; title page and 16 (top) Chris Knapton/ Ecoscene; contents and 35 Ron Giling/
Still Pictures; 4 Nigel Dickinson/ Still Pictures; 5 Hartmut Schwarzbach/ Still Pictures; 6 Thomas Raupach/ Still Pictures; 7 Mark
Edwards/ Still Pictures; 8 Mark Edwards/ Still Pictures; 9 (top) Gayo/ Still Pictures, 9 (right) Dr Gene Feldman/ NASA GSFC/ Science
Photo Library; 10 Nigel Dickinson/ Still Pictures; 11 (right) Mark Edwards/ Still Pictures, 11/12 Rob Bowden/ EASI-Images; 12 (left)
Robert Holmgren/ Still Pictures, 12 (bottom) Isabelle Rouvillois/ Popperfoto/ Reuters; 13 Rob Bowden/ EASI-Images; 14 Paul
Glendell/ Still Pictures; 15 David Reed/ Panos Pictures; 16 (left) Gehl Company/ Corbis; 17 Rob Bowden/ EASI-Images; 18 Paul
Glendell/ Still Pictures; 19 Nigel Dickinson/ Still Pictures; 20 (top) Daniel Dancer/ Still Pictures, 20 (right) Marcus Rose/ Panos
Pictures; 21 Topham Picturepoint; 22 Pictor Uniphoto; 23 Edward Parker/ Still Pictures; 24 (left) Ron Giling/ Still Pictures, 24 (right)
Rob Bowden/ EASI-Images; 25 Joerg Boethling/ Still Pictures; 26 UNEP/ Still Pictures; 27 (top) Edward Parker, 27 (bottom) Alberto
Garcia/ Still Pictures; 28 Ray Roberts/ Ecoscene; 29 (left) Chris Stowers/ Panos Pictures; 29 (right) Herbert Giradet/ Still Pictures; 30
Gordon Clements/ HWPL; 31 (top) Mark Edwards/ Still Pictures, 31 (bottom) Frank Blackburn/ Ecoscene; 32 Topham Picturepoint;
33 Topham Picturepoint; 34 Chapman/ Topham Picturepoint, 34 (inset) Fairtrade Foundation FAIRTRADE Mark; 35 Ron Giling/ Still
Pictures; 36 (top) Topham/ Image Works, 36 (bottom) Toby Adamson/ Still Pictures; 37 Edward Parker; 38 Topham/ Image Works;
39 Nick Cobbing/ Still Pictures; 40 Gerard Fritz/ Eye Ubiquitous; 41 Dylan Garcia/ Still Pictures; 42 Paul Glendell/ Still Pictures; 43
(top) James Davies Travel Photography; 43 (bottom) Guy Stubbs/ Ecoscene; 44 Topham/ Image Works; 45 Bennett Dean/ Eye
Ubiquitous.

LIBRARY OF CONGRESS CATALOGING-IN-PUBLICATION DATA

Bowden, Rob
  Food and Farming / by Rob Bowden.
    p. cm. — (Sustainable world)

Includes bibliographical references and index.

  ISBN 0-7377-1899-4 (hard : alk. paper)

 1. Sustainable development. 2. Farming. 3. Agriculture management.
 4. Food production. I. Title. II. Sustainable world (Kidhaven Press)
    HC79.B69 2004
    338.—dc21

Printed in Hong Kong

Contents

Why sustainable food and farming?

MOST OF YOU READING THIS BOOK will take your food for granted. You'll give relatively little thought to where it comes from or how it is produced and probably even less to where your next meal will come from or even what it will be. For around 14 percent of the world's population, an incredible 800 million people, the situation is very different. They live in hunger, some of them too hungry to work, to learn, even to walk! These people are extremely aware of their food and may go to extraordinary lengths to get their next meal. At the start of the 21st century the world of food and farming is a divided one, and one we should better understand.

This consumer in a U.K. supermarket has an almost endless choice of foods, but many of them will not be produced sustainably.

FEEDING THE WORLD

One explanation given for hunger in the 21st century is the pressure of growing human numbers on the planet's ability to feed them. For over two hundred years scientists and scholars have warned of mass starvations as the world runs short of food. But experience shows that food production has kept pace with population growth, and that, today, there is more food per person than at any time in history. However, globally, food is not distributed evenly, and not everyone has equal access to food, even where it is available. Poverty is one of the main causes of this which means it is the poor who are also the hungry.

DATABANK

To feed everyone estimated to be living in the year 2020, the world's food supply will have to double.

These people, unable to grow or buy their own food, line up for whatever they can get at a famine relief camp in Sudan in 1994.

weblinks

For more information about world hunger, go to www.worldhunger.org

FOOD FOR ALL

In such a world there is an urgent need to change farming systems to ensure that in the future there is food for all. This is especially important given that world population is expected to increase from 6 billion in 1999 to 8 billion by 2028. To meet the needs of 8 billion people food production must increase, but so too must people's ability to access food. Farming methods must also change to protect and conserve the environment on which they depend. This is the idea of sustainable food and farming — providing for the needs of today, without harming the ability of future generations to meet their future needs. This book will explore how sustainable food and farming can, and must, become a reality.

OPINION

…It is incredible to me that farming, the basic industry of mankind, can be in such a state of crisis as it is today. It is an indicator of a society that takes its food for granted, and…it shows how frighteningly detached too many people have become from the reality of how it is actually produced.

Prince Charles, speaking at the 2002 Royal Agricultural Show

The challenges for food and farming

FOR FOOD AND FARMING TO BECOME more sustainable there are several challenges that must be understood. For many of those concerned with food and farming, the greatest challenge has been how to keep pace with the ever expanding human population. Since 1960 the human population has more than doubled, placing great pressure on farming to produce enough food to meet its needs. At a global level, farming has managed this in two main ways — expansion and intensification.

Mechanized farm equipment, such as these combine harvesters in Germany, have had a major influence on the extension of farming land.

FARMING EXPANSION

Expansion simply means the extension of farming systems into new areas that were previously unfarmed. This allows farmers to increase the amount they produce using existing practices. Some of the expansions have been quite dramatic. For example, the global area of grain harvested increased from 1,450,600,000 acres in 1950 to reach 1,809,000,000 by 1981 — an increase of 25 percent.

Although helping to increase food supplies, expansion has often occurred on land that is unsuitable for agriculture.

The exposed roots of this tree show the dramatic effects of soil erosion in Burkina Faso. This is often caused by overgrazing of livestock or the clearance of land for farming.

This marginal land includes areas where soils are infertile, or sloping land where erosion is a major problem. The areas most severely affected by this are often in the poorer, less developed countries where food shortages are most severe. Of the estimated 5,000,000,000 acres of soil degraded (damaged) by human actions since 1945, three-quarters of them lie in less developed regions such as Asia and Africa.

In addition to environmental degradation, expansion has caused the destruction and loss of important areas such as forests, grasslands, and wetlands. It has been estimated for example, that 26 percent of the world's wetlands have been drained to make way for farming — mostly over the last one hundred years. In Europe and North America this estimate rises to 56–65 percent. Such losses are significant as wetlands are home to key animal and plant species. In the United States, 70 percent of its endangered birds and 40 percent of all its endangered species are dependent on wetland environments. Wetlands are also home to numerous important plant species including several types of wild rice that could be a valuable food resource for the future.

DATABANK

The United States is losing wetlands at a rate equivalent to twelve football fields an hour, every day of the year. Most of this is due to farming activities.

These researchers in the Ivory Coast are monitoring new crop varieties at the Rice Research Institute.

INTENSIFICATION

Over the last fifty years advances in farming technology have led to intensification of farming — growing more food on the same area of land. This has allowed food production to keep pace with population growth at a global scale. Between 1981 and 2000 for example, the global grain area shrank by around 9 percent and yet the amount of grain produced increased by 24 percent over the same period.

THE GREEN REVOLUTION

One of the most famous examples of intensification was the Green Revolution that took place in South Asia and Latin America during the 1960s. The Green

DATABANK

The Green Revolution in India increased crop yields from 12 million tons to 23 million tons in just four growing seasons.

Revolution introduced a package of farming chemicals that allowed farmers to increase yields by as much as 50 percent. In the package were new varieties of crops (mainly wheat and rice) known as high-yielding varieties or HYVs. When grown using agricultural chemicals such as fertilizers and pesticides, and irrigation to provide sufficient water, they produced bumper crop yields. The Green Revolution is said to have saved millions of people from hunger and starvation.

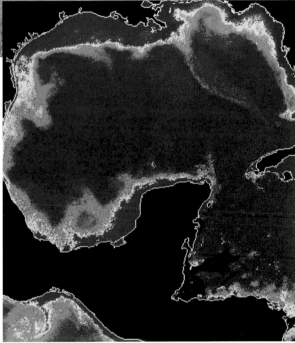

Above: Pesticides are applied to this rice crop in Spain using a helicopter. Much of the pesticide will find its way into the surrounding environment.

Right: The colors in this satellite image of the Gulf of Mexico show algae blooms caused by run off from agricultural fertilizers. Red shows the densest blooms are located close to the land which shows up as black in this image.

The problem with intensive farming methods is that they can have harmful environmental and social effects. For example, most methods involve the heavy use of agricultural chemicals, particularly fertilizers. Since the 1960s, fertilizer use has tripled and continues to grow today. However, up to 85 percent of the fertilizer applied is washed away by rains or irrigation water and finds its way into local water supplies as run off. Here it can encourage rapid plant and algae growth that eventually starves other aquatic life of light and oxygen leading to wide-scale species losses. In the United States, fertilizer run off entering the Mississippi river system has severely reduced seafood harvests in the Gulf of Mexico.

GREAT DIVIDE

Intensification can also create social divides as only wealthier farmers are able to afford all of the necessary chemicals. In India, for example, many poorer farmers were unable to take advantage of the Green Revolution technology, while wealthier landowners were able to further increase their wealth and power. Similar divides have occurred in other countries following the introduction of new farming technology.

APPROACHING THE LIMITS

Expansion and intensification may have avoided wide-scale hunger but they have also provided numerous warnings that current farming methods may be reaching their limits. Erosion, water shortages, soil and water pollution, and declining yields are all signs that the environment can, in many places, no longer support such systems.

LIVESTOCK PRODUCTION

The same is true for other food sources too, such as livestock production. The clearance of land for cattle ranching in Central and South America, for example, is linked to around half of rainforest destruction. In other countries livestock are increasingly competing with humans for both land and food. In fact, in 2000 the world's livestock population of over 20.6 billion used over two-thirds of the world's food-producing land. With some 20 percent of land degraded due to overgrazing, and the demand for meat continuing to expand, efforts to make live-

An area of rainforest in the Amazon is cleared to make way for farming or the ranching of cattle.

Above: These goats lick salt from a hillside that has been eroded by overgrazing in northern Kenya.

Right: Commercial fishing by boats like this sand eel trawler in Denmark has led to some fish stocks being severely reduced.

stock production more sustainable must be found. This is especially important for the estimated 200 million people in the arid (dry) regions of Africa and Central Asia who depend on livestock rearing for the bulk of their food and incomes.

FISH FARMING

Fishing is another source of food that is fast approaching its limits. The global fish catch increased from 19 million tons in 1950 to almost 93 million tons in 1999. A further 33.3 million tons of fish were produced in fish farms — a technique known as aquaculture. This important source of protein is threatened, however,

by severe over-fishing and poor fishing practices. Up to 60 percent of the world's ocean catch is thought to come from areas that are at, or beyond, their limits. With reduced numbers of key species such as cod and blue fin tuna, fishing fleets are increasingly turning to new, and often smaller, varieties of fish as alternatives. Modern fishing trawlers create their own problems, too. Their nets can destroy much of the ocean bed as they drag along the bottom. They also catch almost anything in their path, whether it is wanted or not. Such practices cause the loss of significant species and environmental damage. If this continues it could lead to the collapse of some marine environments.

PLAYING WITH NATURE

The most recent prospects for continued increases in food production come from genetically modified (GM) produce. These are plants and animals that have had their genes (the chemical ingredients that make up all life on earth) manipulated (modified) to improve their growing or food characteristics. For example, fish can be made to grow faster and bigger, or plants to withstand low rainfall or certain diseases. Supporters of GM technology argue that it could bring dramatic increases in food production that would be especially beneficial for food-scarce regions of the world.

The development of GM technology has, however, raised concerns among some scientists and environmentalists. They believe that GM technology is playing with nature and could have unforeseen consequences. They are also concerned about contamination if GM crops and/or animals escape into the wider environment and breed with naturally occurring species. Until more is known about the safety of producing GM foods many of those concerned believe we should be cautious about their use in meeting future food demand.

Left: This U.S. scientist is experimenting with GM technology to try and improve traditional varieties of tomato.

Below: A protestor from Greenpeace holds GM maize that has been removed from a trial field in France. Protestors are concerned that the GM crops will contaminate non-GM crops planted nearby.

Non au maïs transgéniqu...

These women near Lake Naivasha in Kenya pack green beans for export to Europe. Meanwhile, many nearby families are going hungry.

GLOBALLY UNEVEN

Many food experts point out that there is already enough food for everyone in the world, but that it is unevenly distributed. While millions go hungry others enjoy food that has been shipped half way around the world to reach them, sometimes from those same countries where people are going hungry. This reality shows that sustainable food and farming is not just about different technology choices and the environment. It is as much about making sure people have the ability to meet their food needs. This may mean some rethinking of current food distribution and consumption patterns.

In particular, there is growing pressure to reduce the distance that food travels around the world — so-called food miles.

OPINION

Agriculture must help produce not only more food, but also more income and livelihood opportunities.

Professor Monkombu Sambasivan Swaminathan, plant geneticist and winner of 1987 World Food Prize

This is because food transportation contributes to environmental degradation at both a global and local level. Globally, the movement of food uses vast quantities of energy and so contributes to problems associated with global warming. More importantly perhaps, the movement of food can degrade local farming environments as it removes nutrients from the soils that are then transported (as food) hundreds, even thousands of miles away. This means the nutrients are not returned to the environment from where they originated and so the land in that area can quickly become infertile or dependent on chemicals.

Above: An inspector from the Soil Association visits a farm in Derbyshire, United Kingdom. The Soil Association is the organization that approves organic food and farms in the United Kingdom.

Left: This Gehl box muck spreader in the United States applies animal waste to the fields as a form of natural fertilizer.

WORKING WITH NATURE

Intercropping is an example of a farming system that attempts to work with nature. Such systems are considered central to making farming more sustainable and are increasingly being used in the production of our food. Perhaps the best known example of such systems is the growth of the organic farming movement. Organic farming avoids the use of chemicals and produces food using the soil's natural fertility. As in nature, the soils in organic farming are enriched to maintain their fertility by natural fertilizers such as composted plant and animal waste — a method dating back thousands of years.

ORGANIC FARMING

Organic farming is considered a highly sustainable form of farming that respects the environment while still allowing human needs to be met. However, critics of organic farming point out that it is less

DATABANK

Between 1991 and 2001, sales of organic produce in the United States increased by 20 percent per year, making it the fastest growing agricultural sector.

productive than chemically-based farming systems. In a Swiss study for example, yields of wheat were found to be 10 percent lower on organic farms and up to 40 percent lower for potatoes. Because of its lower yields, some experts believe organic farming will never be able to meet the world's growing demand for food. This is especially true for farming in some tropical environments where soils are naturally less fertile and unable to support farming without the use of artificial chemicals.

Despite such concerns, supporters of organic farming argue that it is one of the most efficient and profitable forms of farming. Although yields are lower, the fact that expensive chemicals are not needed more than makes up for this by lowering the costs of production. This could be of particular benefit to many poorer countries that cannot afford expensive chemicals, but have plentiful supplies of labor. In Kenya, for example, several farms have taken advantage of the abundant land and labor supplies to produce organic vegetables for export to high demand markets in Europe. This has created thousands of new jobs in Kenya and in recent years has become one of the country's fastest growing and most important sources of income.

— weblinks, —

For more information about organic food and farming, go to www.ers.usda.gov/briefing/organic

Thousands of jobs have been created in Kenya by the demand for organic vegetables in European markets. This woman is picking organic beans.

The organic produce being sold in this farmers' market in Bath, United Kingdom, is more expensive than non-organic produce, but it does not include the environmental costs.

OPINION

Non-organic food is not as cheap as it appears.

Consumers are paying for it three times over — first over the counter, second via taxation which mainly subsidizes non-organic farming, and third to remedy the damage that farming and food production has done to the environment and human health.

Soil Association, Organic Food and Farming: Myth and Reality

A HIGHER PRICE?

The attitude of food consumers like you and me is important to the development of sustainable farming. Take organic farming, for example. Organic produce is usually more expensive than non-organic (conventional) produce. In a typical U.K. supermarket, a basket of organic vegetables costs around 25–50 percent more than the conventional equivalent. The higher price is seen by some as a barrier to the success of organic and other types of sustainable farming. Those promoting sustainable farming argue that this is misleading. They point out that the higher price paid for organic farming includes not only the higher labor and management costs, but also an amount that goes toward protecting the environment for future generations. The lower price paid for conventional foods does not include the environmental and health costs that are caused by their production — for instance, the cleaning of water courses polluted by chemical fertilizers. Nor does it include the cost of the taxpayers' money that governments often give farmers to produce conventional foods. These payments are known as agricultural or farming subsidies. If these costs were included then conventional foods would cost similar to, if not more than, organic produce.

CONSUMER ATTITUDES

The key concept is that the higher price consumers pay for sustainably produced food is actually a more realistic price that accounts for all of the costs involved in its production. In recent years consumers have shown greater willingness to pay for more sustainably produced food. One of the reasons for this has been a number of high profile food safety concerns that have raised doubts about more conventional farming methods. Among the biggest of these was the case of BSE (Bovine Spongiform Encephalopathy) in the United Kingdom. BSE is a disease found in cattle that have been given feed containing infected meat and bone meal from other animals. In 1996, it was found that BSE could be transferred to humans through eating infected meat products. In humans the disease is known as vCJD (variant Creutzfeldt-Jakob Disease) and is fatal, with no known cure. As a result of BSE, serious questions are now being asked about the way some foods are produced. It is worth noting that there have been no cases of BSE in cattle managed organically since before 1985.

DATABANK
By July 2002, 124 people in the United Kingdom had been diagnosed with Mad Cow Disease, 115 of whom died.

Butchers in the United Kingdom are working hard to restore trust in British beef.

Above: Improved farming technology means large food surpluses are common in some countries. This wheat is being dumped outside because the grain storage silos in the background are already full.

Right: These scientists in Malaysia are using biotechnology to try and improve on existing varieties of banana.

TECHNOLOGY FOR GOOD

With concerns about the safety of food and the sustainability of current farming methods, there is now great interest in trying to find alternatives. Across the world, trials and experiments are taking place to find farming solutions that will both increase food production and better manage the environment. While much of the publicity around sustainable food and farming focuses on more natural methods such as organic farming, the role of technology should not be ignored. Improvements in soil, plant, animal, water and chemical science have enabled scientists to consistently increase crop and animal production over the last fifty years. With genetic science now playing an increasing role, too, science and technology is likely to become even more important in the future.

BIOTECHNOLOGY

Altering the properties of plants, commonly known as biotechnology, has already proved what an improvement it can make to crop yields. However, despite widespread beliefs, it is not true that such benefits are only achievable with the greater use of artificial chemicals. In Mexico, for instance, scientists have developed varieties of wheat that produce higher yields while reducing the need for fertilizers. For example, to produce 5 tons of wheat on a 3-acre plot using wheat varieties from the 1950s, scientists had to add 154 pounds of chemical fertilizers. Using varieties developed in the 1960s and

1970s, this fell to 77 pounds or less. By the 1980s though, new varieties of wheat had been developed that needed no fertilizers at all to produce the same yields. Even when chemicals were used, the new wheat was twice as efficient as the 1950 variety at converting the fertilizer into crop yields, meaning that either way far less chemical fertilizer was now needed.

The concern many experts have about biotechnology is that it only benefits large agricultural companies and already wealthy farmers and countries. The expense of new seed varieties means many poorer farmers cannot afford them. In addition, unlike traditional seeds where a proportion of the harvest can be kept back for planting in the following year, new varieties must often be bought as new seeds every year. This can trap poor farmers into a system where they are at the mercy of the prices charged by the seed companies.

It is often only wealthy farms such as this giant wheat farm in Washington that really benefit from the latest developments in biotechnology.

OPINION

'Raising...crop production by improving plants and fertilizer management is arguably the best way of protecting natural resources...while contributing to the food supplies needed by a growing...population.'

Consultative Group on International Agricultural Research (CGIAR)

Sustainable food and farming in practice

IN REALITY IT IS A COMBINATION OF SCIENTIFIC and more natural methods that is most likely to lead to lasting and sustainable solutions to the world's food and farming needs. Each on their own has several weaknesses, but when used together they can become a powerful force for change. Using examples from around the world, this chapter considers some of the positive solutions already in practice.

Indonesian farmers harvest rice that has been grown using integrated pest management (IPM) techniques to reduce the use of harmful chemical pesticides.

GOOD MANAGEMENT

One of the most promising approaches to sustainable farming is simply to make better use of farm chemicals. Through careful management it is possible to reduce the need for chemicals such as fertilizers, pesticides, and water, and, if they have to be used, to limit their use to an absolute minimum. There are a number of farming systems in use today that follow this approach. They include integrated pest management (IPM) and integrated crop management (ICM).

INTEGRATED PEST MANAGEMENT

A farmer inspects his tomato crop in Sinaloa, Mexico. Farmers in Sinaloa use integrated pest management (IPM) to control pests and improve their yields.

In Sinaloa, Mexico, farmers have been using IPM for over fifteen years to control pests that were attacking the area's tomato crop. The farmers released natural enemies such as insects that feed on the pests and changed their planting methods to disrupt the pests' breeding patterns. Using these methods the use of chemical pesticides was reduced to nothing within just five years. Prior to the use of IPM the tomatoes were being sprayed with different chemical pesticides around forty times per growing season. By the early 1990s tomatoes grown on sites managed with IPM had less crop damage than those growing on non-IPM sites and farmers had increased both their yields and incomes. In Indonesia, a national program to adopt IPM in the cultivation of rice was started in the mid–1980s. As a result, pesticide use in Indonesia fell by 60 percent and rice harvests increased by a quarter.

INTEGRATED CROP MANAGEMENT

Integrated crop management (ICM) has proven just as successful as IPM and by using a variety of techniques it has reduced the use of artificial chemicals considerably. Crop rotation is one such technique that involves alternating the type of crop grown each season. By doing this, pests or diseases that feed on any particular crop are given less chance of surviving into the next season because their food source is removed.

Above: This Sri Lankan woman can earn income from the sale of her avocado pears — a delicious and very nutritious fruit.

Right: A nursery attendant in Kenya cares for seedlings that will be sold to local farmers for use in agroforestry projects.

AGROFORESTRY

The use of trees in more sustainable farming practices may not be obvious, but trees do in fact provide many benefits. For example, their root systems help to bind soils together and so reduce erosion. Their canopy can provide shade for crops or animals in hot countries, and when planted in certain ways they can act as a windbreak to reduce crop damage. Certain species of tree also have additional benefits such as improving the quality of the soils or providing fruits or leaves that can be eaten by people or their animals. Farming with trees in this way is known as agroforestry.

The multiple benefits of agroforestry make it an especially attractive form of sustainable farming as it not only helps protect environments and increase food production, but also provides incomes for the rural poor. Fruit trees are especially valuable. In Africa, farmers that plant mango, avocado, or banana trees for example, may increase their incomes by up to ten times. By improving incomes as well as food production, farmers are better able to withstand crop failures caused by drought or disease because they can sell their tree products to buy food. In Malawi, in 2002, during a severe drought and food shortages the only farmers still able to feed themselves were the estimated twenty-two thousand families using agroforestry techniques.

THE NEEM TREE

The Neem tree is just one species that has numerous benefits for farmers in hot tropical countries. It is a leguminous tree, meaning it is able to fix nitrogen from the air and improve the fertility of soils. It produces nutritious seeds that are a useful source of fodder for animals such as goats, and it grows rapidly meaning it can provide fuelwood for poor rural families in just a few years. Its bark and leaves are known to repel mosquitoes and so if planted close to settlements can help reduce cases of malaria (a disease transmitted by mosquitoes). It is also said to have numerous medicinal benefits and in parts of Kenya is used by local healers to treat around forty different complaints.

This farmer in Rajasthan, India, collects fuelwood from a Neem tree.

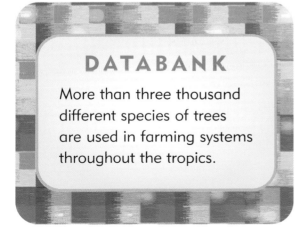

DATABANK

More than three thousand different species of trees are used in farming systems throughout the tropics.

AQUACULTURE

Aquaculture is the raising of fish, or other water-dependent foods such as shellfish and seaweed, in an artificial environment. There is little new about aquaculture. In fact its origins can be traced back around three thousand years to China where fish were kept in small farm ponds as part of a highly sustainable system. This technique is still used today. Various species of carp are the most commonly kept fish. They are raised in ponds located on farms that normally grow crops and/or keep animals too. The system is highly efficient and recycles waste from one part of the farm to another. For example, pig manure may be added to the ponds as a natural fertilizer. This promotes the growth of plankton on which the carp feed. The waste sediment from the bottom of the fish pond is in turn removed as a rich natural fertilizer for the farmer's crops, reducing or removing the need to use chemicals.

This system is so successful that it is now practised in countries around the world such as India, Bangladesh, Vietnam, Zambia, Kenya and Malawi. In Indonesia an incredible 78 percent of farming families keep fish in small on-farm ponds. One of the main benefits of such methods is that it provides poor farmers with a good source of protein, essential for their general health and well-being. In fact fish provides the main source of protein for around 1 billion of the world's people!

These commercial fish farms are in China, the world leader in aquaculture. In 2000, China accounted for two-thirds of world production.

DATABANK

Aquaculture, the farming of fish, shellfish, seaweeds, and the like, represents the fastest growing sector in world food production.

OPINION

Fish farming is not a solution to the world food problem, but as China has demonstrated, it does offer a potential source of low-cost animal protein for lower income populations.

Lester Brown, President,
Earth Policy Institute

Above: These fish ponds in Hunan Province, China, are surrounded by ridges on which farmers grow two crops of rice and one of oilseed rape (the crop now growing) every year.

Left: Fish provides an important source of protein to many of the world's poorest communities. This meal being prepared in the Philippines is using fish that were too small to sell in the market.

RICE-FISH FARMING

Research institutes are now working with farmers to try and further improve traditional aquaculture methods so that they can contribute even more food in the future. In parts of China, for example, experiments began in the mid–1980s to improve the practice of rice-fish farming. This is where fish are raised in the flooded paddy fields used to grow rice. The fish help to control rice pests such as the golden snail and help fertilize the soils. In Guizhou province farmers now farm rice and fish in ridge-ditch fields instead of the traditional flat paddies. In ridge-ditch fields, the rice grows on the ridge of soil with the fish living in the flooded ditches in between. This simple adaptation increased yields of rice by around 18 percent and fish yields grew by an amazing 172 percent.

---

weblinks

For more information about aquaculture, go to www.was.org

DATABANK

The transportation of food accounted for almost 40 percent of all freight traffic on the United Kingdom's roads in 2001.

Local farmers' markets such as this one in Amiens, France, are increasing in popularity as people look to reduce the distance their food has traveled.

FOOD MILES

Improved transportation and food technology (especially food preservation techniques) mean that farming has become less locally based. It has become a truly global industry. Food can travel immense distances before it reaches consumers, and this has been given a name — food miles. Of particular concern is that, as the food industry becomes less localized, these food miles are increasing. In the United Kingdom for example, the distance food travels by road increased by 50 percent between 1978 and 1999. Food miles by ship, and increasingly by air, are also rising. In fact, a recent study showed that using various forms of transport a traditional meal purchased from a U.K. supermarket may have traveled over 24,000 miles! The same study shows that if purchased locally a similar meal would involve over sixty times fewer food miles, and therefore use fifty times less energy.

GOING LOCAL

Local food markets help to reduce these food miles. They also encourage farmers to produce more of the food that is in local demand and help consumers to become more in touch with where and how their food is produced. In less developed countries, local markets remain a major source of food for millions of people. In many African countries, for example, permanent or weekly markets are the focus of community life providing not only food, but also a place for farmers to share their knowledge and ideas about farming. In recent years consumer demands for more local and freshly produced food mean that local markets are becoming increasingly popular in more developed regions, too. In the United States the number of local farmers' markets in-creased by 63 percent to over 2,800 between 1994 and 2000.

Urban agriculture is another way in which food and farming is becoming more local. Using available urban spaces to grow food can improve local food availability, improve the quality of the environment, and put people directly in touch with the land and their food. In Europe, allotments (small pieces of owned or rented land), have long been a feature of urban areas and contributed to local needs. In Copenhagen, Denmark, urban farming is being promoted by one suburb to make the region self sufficient in food by 2005. Families are encouraged to grow vegetables in their gardens, to keep chickens or to join community livestock schemes where a number of families own and manage cattle or sheep on plots of rented farmland.

weblinks

For more information about urban agriculture, go to www.urbanag.tamu.edu

OPINION

With over half the world's people expected to live in cities by 2005, ensuring regular supplies of safe and affordable food will be one of the key food . . . issues of the future.

Food and Agriculture Organization (FAO)

Below, left: This urban farmer is preparing his land in Jakarta, Indonesia. This scene provides a stark contrast to the central business district in the background.

Below, right: Small urban gardens known as allotments have long been popular in the United Kingdom. During World War II they provided a vital supply of food as part of a campaign called Dig For Victory.

These rice farmers in China use terracing to protect and conserve the hillsides and soils. This technique dates back many hundreds of years.

sustainable food and farming system should recognize this and support farmers to better manage and conserve the environment for future generations to enjoy. Farmers themselves are often among the first to recognize when the environment is suffering as a result of human activities. In the Philippines, for example, fishing communities have set up no-take reserves in the region's over-fished coral reefs. These reserves have a breeding zone in which fishing is completely banned and an area around them (a buffer zone) in which fishing is strictly limited. Within just three years both the variety and the number of fish had improved and fishing yields in the waters surrounding the no-take reserves increased significantly. The movement has now spread to nearby Indonesia.

In Europe, farmers can now apply for money from their governments to create areas (habitats) on their farms in which wild species can live and breed. In the United Kingdom, for example, 658,000 acres of land is now part of a national Countryside Stewardship Scheme (CSS). Over ten thousand farmers have been given grants to restore land to its natural state. As well as whole areas, farmers are

ENVIRONMENTAL MANAGERS

An often forgotten, but important, part played by farmers is their role in managing the environment. The methods they choose to adopt have a direct influence on the state of the environment and the wildlife it supports. A more

OPINION

We want [the public] to support the principle that farmers should be paid for providing benefits that they can enjoy — whether this is as a stunning view, or a field full of native flowers.

Sue Cornwell, Senior Countryside Officer, U.K. Countryside Agency

Under the U.K. Country Stewardship Scheme (program), farmers can receive grants to help them rebuild traditional countryside features such as stone walls.

also paid for restoring traditional hedgerows and stone walls around their fields. These provide an important habitat for wildlife such as birds and small mammals. By 2000, nine years after the start of the CSS some 995 miles of walls and nearly 9,320 miles of hedgerows had been restored.

In many poorer countries, it may be impossible for governments to fund such environmental management plans, especially if they are suffering a shortage of food supplies at the same time. Despite such problems, many experts believe that by encouraging farmers to better manage the environment, they will benefit from higher yields in the longer term. Maintaining hedgerows (or boundaries) for example, can help reduce soil erosion and crop damage from high winds. The benefits of environmental management mean that it is likely to make an important contribution to the future of sustainable food and farming.

This English meadow has blossomed on land that has been set aside under a European plan to control the spread of farming.

Making food and farming sustainable

CREATING A FUTURE IN WHICH FOOD and farming is sustainable will need more than just new technologies or alternative farming practices. It will also need the support and action of governments, institutions and individuals. In fact, many experts argue that such political and social changes are even more important than the progress being made in technology and farming practices.

Subsidies paid to European farmers mean that crops are frequently over-produced. This French farmer adds his apples to others that will be wasted as a result.

LEADING THE WAY

Many food campaigners believe that governments should take a lead role in promoting sustainable food and farming but, to date, they have been relatively slow to act. Where they have acted it has normally been by introducing financial penalties or incentives for farmers to change their practices. In Denmark, for example, the government has introduced a system whereby farmers must calculate their use of nitrogen fertilizers to make them balance with the crops' needs. If they exceed the allowable levels then the farmer must pay a fine. In neighboring Sweden, the introduction of a 7.5 percent tax on pesticides led to a reduction in pesticide use of around 65

OPINION

In [the] future, farmers will not be paid for overproduction, but for responding to what people want — safe food, quality production, animal welfare and a healthy environment.

Franz Fischler,
EU Agriculture Commissioner

The Florida Everglades are among the wetlands that are now better protected following the introduction of the Swampbuster policy.

percent. And in the United States, the so-called Swampbuster policy was introduced to reduce the loss of America's wetlands. Farmers who ignore the policy and continue to convert wetlands for farming will have any financial support from the government taken away.

While such measures are welcome, campaigners argue that governments should be doing more to directly support sustainable food and farming. Each year, governments in the more developed regions give billions of dollars to farmers, most of whom continue to farm using conventional methods. In the European Union (EU) alone, these payments (subsidies) amount to some $44 billion a year. Now, say supporters of sustainable farming, it is time for governments to start encouraging sustainable practices and improved environmental management instead. Campaign groups such as the U.K.–based Sustain are playing an important role in persuading governments and the public that such changes are long overdue. Sustain is an alliance of over one hundred different groups involved in sustainable food and farming around the world. By working together they can promote their causes more widely and join forces to lobby governments to make changes to existing policies and practices.

— weblinks —

For more information about Sustain, go to www.sustainweb.org

DATABANK

Over five hundred thousand small-scale coffee growers benefited from the fair trade system in 2002.

FAIRTRADE

Guarantees a **better deal** for Third World Producers

Clear labeling and information about Fairtrade products helps consumers to make choices that will support farmers in less developed countries.

FAIR TRADING

The current world trading system works against small-scale and poor farmers, particularly in Asia, Africa, and South America. These farmers find it hard to compete internationally because of the power and support that farming in more developed regions such as North America and Europe receive. The subsidies paid to farmers in these regions encourage them to overproduce and so the world markets can become quickly flooded with surplus food stocks. When this happens, world food prices are forced down. Farmers in less developed regions may find it hard to survive on the lower prices they receive for their produce. More worrying than low prices, however, is the uncertainty of world prices. They can rise and fall dramatically from year to year, making it especially hard for farmers to plan for their futures.

This unstable situation is now being addressed by a number of organizations that are promoting fair trade for farmers in less developed countries. Fair trade works by offering farmers a guaranteed price for their produce that covers the costs of sustainable production and living. The price is agreed with the farmer at an early stage and they can be paid a proportion of the price in advance to help support their families in the period leading up to the harvest. In addition, farmers are paid a premium (an extra amount) for investing in long-term development such as education or healthcare.

The fair trade system removes the uncertainty of fluctuating world prices and encourages investment in poor rural economies. In 2002 fair trade produce came from thirty-six countries and was for sale in seventeen, including the United Kingdom, Denmark, the United States, and Japan. In many of these countries fair trade products are now becoming leading brands. In Switzerland, for example, one in every five bananas sold is a fair trade banana, and fair trade ground coffee accounts for around 7 percent of the U.K. ground coffee market. Across the seventeen countries selling fair trade products, sales increased by 21 percent in 2001. Millions of farmers already benefit from fair trade and with such growth in sales of their produce it is hoped that millions more will benefit in the coming years.

OPINION

"Paying Fairtrade prices will get rid of the uncertainty of farmers, who are being driven out by high production costs. It would help in a real way with education and keeping the rural economy alive."

Renwick Rose, Windward Islands National Farmers Association (WINFA)

weblinks

For more information about the Fairtrade Foundation, go to www.fairtrade.org

These women are packing organic Fairtrade bananas in Ghana, ready for export to Europe. The Fairtrade agreement ensures that workers are paid fairly.

Top: This French shopper is assured that her pineapple is organically grown by the labeling system used.

Above: Without the benefit of consumer labeling plans products such as this fairly traded cocoa from Ghana would be difficult to sell.

MAKING IT CLEAR

One of the main reasons for the success of fair trade produce is its highly effective labeling program. All fair trade products are sold with a recognizable logo or label that identifies them as being different to normally traded produce. The labeling program allows consumers to quickly identify those products that meet the fair trade standards.

Labels are an important part of making sustainable food and farming work. Consumers need information about where and how different foods are produced, and labels provide a quick and easy way for this information to be presented. Some labeling, such as where a product originates from, is relatively simple. Developing labels that tell us whether a product is produced sustainably or not is more of a challenge. Despite this, many sustainable farming practices have been successful in establishing their own labeling systems. In the United Kingdom for example, organic produce is often marked with the logo of The Soil Association — an organization that monitors and certifies organic produce on behalf of the consumer. A similar plan was introduced by the U.S. Department for Agriculture (USDA) in October 2002 to help support the growing organic market in the United States.

MARINE STEWARDSHIP COUNCIL

One of the most interesting labeling programs is that of the Marine Stewardship Council (MSC). The MSC monitors the global fishing industry and labels fish products that have been caught using sustainable practices that offer protection to fish stocks and their environments. By 2002, the MSC logo was being used in over twenty countries and was supported by more than one hundred organizations involved in the fishing industry. What makes the MSC labeling program particularly interesting, however, is the fact that it was set up in 1996 by one of the world's biggest food corporations — Unilever — in partnership with WWF (World Wildlife Fund), one of the world's leading conservation organizations. This new era of cooperation between international businesses and conservation groups is a good sign for the future of sustainable food and farming because it is large food corporations like Unilever that control much of the current world trade in food.

---

weblinks

For more information about the Marine Stewardship Council, go to www.msc.org

---

This fisherman is landing mackerel caught by line and hook. Such methods are approved by the Marine Stewardship Council as they help to preserve stocks.

TAKING RESPONSIBILITY

The actions of the food corporations (large food producers, or buyers and sellers such as supermarkets) are vital to the future of food and farming. As the main buyers and sellers of food these corporations have enormous power to influence both individual farmers and indeed entire governments. They buy food in enormous quantities and are able to source their supplies from almost anywhere in the world. With such influence, many food campaigners are urging corporations to take greater responsibility for the way in which the food they purchase and sell to customers is produced. If corporations began to change their purchasing in favor of sustainable farming then their suppliers (the farmers) would have to adapt their practices to meet these new demands.

There are signs that such corporate responsibility is beginning to take effect. In the United Kingdom, for example, one leading supermarket chain is encouraging its suppliers to adopt more sustainable practices. Its activities include trading agreements with Caribbean banana gro-

As consumers we can influence the sustainability of food and farming every time we go food shopping.

Campaigners outside the National Farmers' Union offices in the United Kingdom protest against the introduction of GM foods which have been nick-named Frankenfoods.

wers, the promotion of organic produce and support for livestock farmers involved in environmental management plans.

CONSUMER POWER

Though corporations may have great power, it is given to them by their customers — people like you and me. As consumers become more aware of how and where their food is produced, they can force corporations to respond to their demands. If corporations fail to act then customers may stop buying their products causing their business to suffer as a result. A good example of how consumers can influence corporations is the movement against genetically modified (GM) foods in much of Europe. With concerns about the safety of GM foods, many cor-

OPINION

In today's world a business leader must be an environmental leader as well.

Jack Greenberg, McDonald's Chairman & Chief Executive Officer

porations have had to react to consumer worries and remove GM foods from sale. For example, the French supermarket chain, Carrefour, now guarantees that none of its own-brand products contain GM ingredients. Similar actions are being taken by corporations across Europe. The EU now has a law that all food items containing more than 1 percent GM ingredients must say so on the packaging. The impact of the anti-GM campaign in Europe is a clear indication that individuals consumers also have a role to play.

Sustainable food and farming and you

YOU MIGHT THINK YOU have few connections with the places and the people who produce much of the food you eat. When we buy food from the supermarket or local store it is sometimes easy to forget that somebody somewhere makes their livelihood out of producing it. By making an effort to think about where and how our food is produced we can all make a positive contribution toward more sustainable food and farming.

The information given on food labels can tell us what foods contain. They also increasingly tell us where and how they were produced.

THINK BEFORE YOU BUY

The key message from sustainable food campaigners is to think before you buy. In the past it has been difficult to shop with knowledge, but new labeling programs, such as those mentioned in the previous chapter, have made it easier to identify where food has come from and how it was produced. One of the problems facing consumers, however, is the fact that several different factors may influence their decision. For example, you may decide that the health and environmental benefits of organic farming make you want to buy organic produce. But you may also have to take into account where

A farmers' market in London provides shoppers with the opportunity to support local farmers and buy organic.

OPINION

We need to invest, now, in regional and local food systems combined with fair trade initiatives that will bring about a more secure, sustainable and fair food system.

Andy Jones, Eating Oil: Food Supply in a Changing Climate, *2001*

that organic food has come from. In the United Kingdom, for instance, around 70 percent of organic food comes from abroad and has often traveled thousands of food miles. A basket of twenty-six imported organic products may have traveled a combined distance of an incredible 150,000 miles — equivalent to six times around the world! In addition to those decisions you may also want to know whether the farmers producing that product are being fairly paid and treated. And, of course, price is also important, especially if you are shopping within a budget like many families and individuals around the world.

DAZED AND CONFUSED

With so many choices to make, supporting sustainable farming each time you go food shopping can leave you feeling rather dazed and confused. Food campaign groups are working hard to make such choices easier. Their efforts have for example, persuaded many super-markets to have exclusive organic sections in their stores, making it easier for those customers who wish to support organic food and farming. In many instances though, supporting sustainable food and farming means knowing what to look out for and how to make a difference.

41

Vegetable Box programs provide a service in many communities where fresh organic produce is brought door to door.

LOCAL ACTION
Doing your part

- Shop with a conscience — think about where your food comes from and the impact it has had on people and the environment.

- If you are not sure about certain foods then ask the store for the information you want.

- Look for local produce to support your local farmers and reduce food miles.

- Find out about local farmers' markets or doorstep delivery programs for local produce.

- If you have a garden, or access to land, then look into the possibility of growing food yourself.

- Raise the issue of food and farming at school. You could start a school vegetable garden or try to arrange a trip to a sustainable farm.

- Share with others what you have learned from reading this book.

TAKING ACTION

Food producers and sellers depend on consumers for their livelihoods. That means that if consumers begin to demand changes in the way the food they eat is produced and sold then producers will have to listen. It is sometimes easy to forget that you have that power as a consumer, but on the left are a few ways in which you can begin taking action.

A WAY OF LIFE

Many people are discouraged from taking action because of the expense or time involved. Supporters argue that it does not take long to adjust to a slightly different way of life. They argue that the little extra you pay is not just for your food, but for conserving the environment for your own children, and even grandchildren, to enjoy in the future. Taking action can also be personally rewarding. Growing your own food can be a very satisfying experience and it need not take up much space either. Even a small window box can be used to grow herbs. It is easy to make a difference if we are prepared to make the effort.

Right: A greenhouse can make growing your own food, such as tomatoes, a simple and enjoyable activity.

Below: These young South Africans are getting a firsthand experience of growing their own food in a community gardening program.

The future of sustainable food and farming

FOOD AND FARMING IS A COMPLEX industry that in some way involves every single person on the planet. For millions, their lives depend on their ability to farm their land successfully. But for the millions of others living in the world's rapidly growing cities, food has become largely separated from the production process.

Buying food from local farmers' markets such as this one in Jacksonville, Florida, allows consumers to talk with farmers about the challenges facing food and farming.

Small-scale farmers like this one in Vietnam have developed many years of expertise that will be vital in creating more sustainable food and farming methods in the future.

TAKE IT PERSONALLY

People rarely understand where their food has come from and how it has been produced. They are probably unaware of the negative effects that many farming practices have on the environment, on wildlife, and on human health. And they are probably even less aware of the alternative ideas and practices (many of which already exist) that could make our food and farming more sustainable.

The examples in this book show that there is much that can be done to make food and farming more sustainable. They show that rather than panic about a world running short of food, it is time to think again about the way in which food and farming is organized and managed. Trading systems must be made fairer, especially to allow poor farmers in less developed regions to rise out of poverty — the main cause of hunger in the world today. We must learn to better respect the environment which produces our food and be prepared to pay the price for its management and conservation for future generations.

Perhaps most importantly we should recognize the essential role that farmers play, not only in producing our food, but in managing the environment. They have built up a great knowledge of how to survive and prosper from the land that gives us our food. In the struggle for a more sustainable future, their knowledge will be essential, but they will also require the support of governments, corporations and individuals. It is up to each of us to become better connected to our food and the environments from which it comes. It is only through taking it personally, and making the appropriate decisions, that sustainable food and farming can become a reality for a sustainable world.

Glossary

Agroforestry The growing of trees and agricultural crops alongside each other. The trees shade the crops and can help to improve soil quality.

Aquaculture The farming of marine and freshwater fish, animals, and plants for human consumption.

Biotechnology The manipulation of plant and animal species and soil, water, and chemical cycles in order to increase yields. More recently this also includes modifying genes using genetic engineering.

BSE (Bovine Spongiform Encephalopathy) A disease that affects cattle, also known as mad cow disease. If infected meat products are eaten, BSE may be transferred to humans in the form of vCJD (variant Creutzfeldt-Jakob Disease) which is fatal with no known cure.

Canopy A covering or shelter provided by the upper branches and leaves of a tree.

Erosion A process whereby something becomes worn (eroded). For example, the removal of material (soil or rock) by the forces of nature (wind or rain) or by people (deforestation, vehicle tracks, etc.).

Expansion An increase in size or area. Used in farming to describe the growth of farming onto land not previously cultivated.

Fair trade Trade that ensures producers are paid a fair (and often guaranteed) price for their produce. Coffee, tea, bananas, and chocolate are among the Fairtrade products available in many supermarkets.

Food miles A value that represents the distance, in miles, that food is transported to reach consumers. Consuming locally grown/produced food ensures the fewest food miles.

Food security The ability to meet essential food needs by producing food or having sufficient money to purchase food.

Global warming The gradual warming of the earth's atmosphere as a result of greenhouse gases, such as carbon dioxide and methane, trapping heat.

GM foods Foodstuffs that have had their genes changed (genetically modified) in order to improve their productivity or another quality, such as taste and color.

Integrated crop management (ICM) The management of different crops in such a way that the need for chemicals is reduced or eliminated.

Integrated pest management (IPM) The use of biological controls and changes in planting patterns to reduce or eliminate the use of chemical pesticides.

Intensification Growing or raising more food without an increase in the area farmed.

Intercropping A system of growing several crops together in such a way that each benefits the other.

Leguminous plants Plants that attract microscopic bacteria that are able to absorb nitrogen from the atmosphere and transfer or fix it into the soil. This practice reduces the need for the application of nitrogen fertilizers. Peas, beans, and groundnuts are among the most widely grown leguminous plants.

For further exploration

Marginal land Areas of land that are less suited to cultivation. They may have poor quality soils or be on sloping ground or in valleys prone to flooding.

Organic farming Farming or raising livestock without using artificial chemicals. Yields are often lower, but organic produce is said to be safer for human consumption and to be less damaging to the environment.

Overgrazing Permanent loss of vegetation due to animals grazing faster than vegetation can re-grow. This usually happens where too many animals graze a limited area of land.

Pesticides Chemicals used to kill insects and pests.

Protein An element of food essential for human health and especially important for healthy bones and blood. Meat, fish, eggs, and beans are all high protein foods.

Subsidy A payment, normally made by governments, to encourage certain practices.

Sustainable food and farming The production of food using practices that provide for the needs of today's population while protecting the environment so that future generations can meet their needs.

Wetlands An area of marsh or swamp where the soil is saturated with water like a sponge.

Yield The total amount of crops grown in a measured area (normally an acre) per year.

Books

Rob Bowden, *21st Century Debates: Food Supply.* London: Hodder Wayland, 2002.

Nigel Hawkes, *Saving Our World: Genetically Modified Food.* London: Franklin Watts, 2000.

Sally Morgan and Pauline Lalor, *Sustainable Future: World Food.* London: Franklin Watts, 1997.

Catherine Paladino, *One Good Apple: Growing Our Food for the Sake of the Earth.* Boston: Houghton Mifflin, 1999.

Index